The Sky Is
Where My Heart Is

── Dream High, Fly High ──

Jean Jiyoung Lee

To order additional copies of this book, contact:
Xlibris
844-714-8691
www.Xlibris.com
Orders@Xlibris.com

ISBN: Softcover   978-1-6698-0908-1
          EBook   978-1-6698-0907-4

Print information available on the last page

Rev. date: 01/31/2022

To my beloved mother, who is Kim in this biography.
She has always been my number one inspiration
and trustworthy anchor in life. Also, this book is a
reminder of my deepest love for my father in Heaven
and my loving older sister, Boyoung Diane Lee.

Acknowledgments

Huge gratitude goes to my husband, Youngjin, and our one and only son, Hans, neither of whom have frowned upon my crazy running obsession, silly behavior, or wish to do whatever's on my mind. I love you, and thank you for your constant support and trust in me.

I would also like to extend my deepest thanks to Mr. Wayne Robert Miller, who used to teach my son in middle school and who has become his lifelong mentor and my close friend. Without his support and friendship, I would never have been able to start the process of writing this book. Additionally, I am grateful to have Professor Lia Kamhi-Stein from my graduate school who first encouraged me to write a story of my mother's life for young readers with big dreams. She helped me believe that my mother's life story would have a positive impact on promising children like her own fifteen-year-old daughter, Hannah.

My friend, Patty Caudill, should certainly be mentioned here—not only as my loving friend, but also as a wonderful mother of three beautiful children: Jake, Jessica, and Joe.

Last but not least, I feel so grateful for the team at Xlibris Publishing who helped me through the process of publication.

Chapter 1
Kim's Childhood

To Kim, who did not have a toy to play with, trees and streams in the small town made perfect playgrounds. She ran around, climbed the trees, and sat on the branches all day long.

Kim loved looking up at the sky so much. She would wonder, *Who is living in those clouds? Is it warm or cold? How did someone get all the way up there?* Little Kim was hungry but happy, daydreaming about playing with the sky. She would sometimes visualize herself soaring up on those clouds and jumping from one fluffy cloud to another.

Kim had been born to a poor family in a small town in North Korea. Her mom and dad worked in the fields all the time. When Kim was born in 1934, she had two older brothers and two older sisters. Then came another younger brother and two younger sisters after Kim.

It was hard for Mom and Dad to keep each child in check or even see if they had eaten anything throughout a day. Kim's sisters and brothers were always making a lot of noise running around their small house, but Kim stayed quiet and played all by herself. Nothing seemed to amuse this little girl, except when she had a chance to see a bird flying high into the sky until it flew out of her sight.

Chapter 2
Kim's School Days

When Kim was in elementary school she was not an active student, but rather a very quiet girl who stayed in the back of her classroom. Since her parents were busy and poor, Kim was not able to bring lunch or even a morsel of something to munch on during the day. She ran around the playground and drank water from the well while most of her friends enjoyed their lunches.

There was a big tree in the school playground that was Kim's favorite. She would climb all the way to the top. That was her happy place where she could enjoy the blue sky. Each time she looked up at the clouds in the sky, her imagination was full, just as it had been in her childhood. Her mind was full of questions. *If someone is living up there, how did that person get there?* When Kim was imagining or dreaming of someone living in the skies, she forgot that she was hungry every day.

The classroom was not a cozy place for Kim. She was always the one being scolded and given time-outs by her teachers because she had forgotten to bring pencils or textbooks to school. Kim was sometimes even pulled from her seat and told to stand alone in the back corner of the classroom. She felt unhappy, but nothing compared to her wild imagination about somebody living up there in the skies.

She grew up without feeling cared or dearly loved by her parents. There were too many children for the poor parents to pay full attention to each one. Monotonous days passed by until Kim had a special awakening moment in high school. The principal at her school told the students about the Korean Air Force Academy and their decision to seek girls who wanted to join as the first women cadets in the Republic of Korea.

When Kim broke the exciting news from her school principal to her parents, they were furious. The first thing Kim heard from Mom and Dad was, "Are you crazy? You are joining the air force academy? That is a man's job!" When Kim kept saying how wonderful it would be to fly, her parents gave her a stern look.

"OK, go ahead. Then you will be disowned from our family!" they said.

Kim felt disappointed, but she secretly applied for the cadet recruit and took the entrance examination.

A few days later, her father was furious to find out in the newspaper that his daughter had made it into the air force academy.

Kim was included in the list of girls who had passed the entrance examination. She was forced to be grounded at home, and her parents locked her in her room on the day of the first meeting of successful cadet candidates.

Chapter 3
Kim Joins the Air Force Academy

Although Kim had been confined to her room for days, her mind was already running out there to the place where trucks were waiting for the candidates who'd passed the entrance exam for the air force academy. Kim was not able to sleep or eat well in her own cozy room. She kept thinking, *I need to get there! I want to join the air force academy! Yes, I will become a pilot!* She finally stood up, opened the window, and jumped out onto the small yard of her house. She turned around and said in a low voice, "Mom, Dad, sisters, and brothers, I am so sorry. But I need to go! I really need to go now! Stay well!"

With a small sheet of map crumpled in her hand, she was running as hard and fast as she could to the place for the candidates to join the air force academy. She wasn't even aware when she lost one of the shoes she'd borrowed from her friend's house on her way to get to the meeting place. When she arrived, she was completely soaked in sweat. Kim found a couple of trucks right there. She was out of breath when asked if she was one of the cadet candidates. The truck took Kim and other cadet candidates to Kimpo Air Force Base, where they were trained to be pilots.

★★★

The first thing to be done was getting a haircut. The girls, including Kim, had to wear a short crew cut, just like the male soldiers. What Kim saw in the mirror was not just a girl or a boy with short hair, but a young person with a dream to fly in the sky. She was strongly determined not to put herself in a box that would limit or define what a woman should or should not do in her own country.

She and her fellow cadets were in harsh training day and night. Two years into the training to become a pilot, the Korean War broke out in 1950. While male pilots were on the fast track of intensive training to be sent out to fight against North Korea, all female cadets were left out, with no chance to participate in any of those trainings. Fourteen of the fifteen woman cadets quit and left the air force academy. Kim was the only one who remained.

The more she felt quietly pressured to leave the academy, the more determined she was to become a pilot. Two years into the Korean War, she was finally chosen to complete the duty of her first solo flight of fifty hours. It was ten o'clock in the morning, October 12, 1952, when Kim was assigned to fly all by herself. The first thing she did was write a letter, which could be the last words in her life to her parents. Also, as pilots normally did, Kim put her nail clippings in the envelope to leave behind along with the letter.

She took a deep breath to stay in control and poised right before she took her first step to fly alone into the sky. Kim finished the fifty hours of her first solo flight with fear, tension, sweat, and concentration. As she landed and stepped out of the plane, there were many newspaper reporters and photographers waiting for the first official woman pilot in the Republic of Korea.

Chapter 4
Kim Goes to America.

After her intensive training and fifty hours of solo flights were completed, Kim was assigned to become a liaison officer. It was tough to play the role of a messenger who provided communication and delivered confidential documents. In those days, when military service was believed to be only for men, Kim's life in the air force was not an easy one. However, not a day passed without her dreaming of flying high into the sky—even if it meant flying in a different country.

When the Korean War ended in an armistice in 1953, President Lee Seongman of the Republic of Korea was planning to promote and develop the field of civil aviation and aeronautics. As an air force captain, Kim was offered a golden opportunity to study aeronautics and civil aviation in the United States as a government-funded student. She left for America in 1958 with her soaring dream to fly high and become a more knowledgeable pilot.

The first place Kim landed in America was Greensboro, North Carolina. She was scheduled to practice flying with trainers on the site of a local airport there. Since she could hardly speak or understand English, she started to learn in the English as a Second Language (ESL) program at Guilford College.

When she first arrived in the US, Kim's English was little more than the ability to say *yes or no*, *thank you*, and *my name is Kyung-O Kim*. One funny episode happened when she was going to grab something to eat from the dorm fridge. Her friends asked her where she was heading, and Kim said she was going to the *chicken*, rather than the *kitchen*. Since she was shy and ashamed of her awkward English, she used to pick only bananas and milk at the student cafeteria so she didn't have to say a lot of words. To make matters worse, she was trying to save money by skipping meals, which put her in a state of malnutrition. Thus, she was told not to practice flying at the airport for several months until she became physically healthy again.

During the unexpected hiatus from flight training, Kim was doing part-time work at the airport. She was washing light aircrafts, which was as hard as it could be, so that those planes would be perfectly ready for the next flights. Besides this work in the airport, Kim was doing other part-time jobs that she could do with her limited English.

She tried babysitting a toddler, but she could hardly understood even the young child. When the toddler's mom came home to find her young one crying, she threw a couple of quarters onto the floor and yelled, "You're fired!"

As Kim picked up those coins from the floor, she was humiliated, but she felt better when she thought about tomorrow, when she would fly again.

★★★

During Kim's long summer break, she worked at an ice cream parlor at Jones Beach in New York. Again, her lack of proficiency with English got in the way of her work. Customers wanted all different kinds of ice cream with a variety of toppings and syrups. Since Kim was not able to catch their fast-paced orders, she just gave everyone exactly the same thing: two scoops of vanilla on a cone. She didn't keep that job long either.

Even though Kim was lonely and homesick, she was not sad because of her dream and passion to become a pilot and the incredible joy of learning developed civil aviation in America.

Kyung Kim Will Be On CBS Television Next Tuesday Night

The news that a young Asian woman pilot had come to the United States traveled fast. Many newspapers and TV broadcast stations contacted Guilford College, wanting to interview Kim. (Refer to the Guilfordian paper on Kim's news about her TV show appearance).

Kim made it on the famous CBS TV panel show *What's My Line*?. It was rare and very interesting for an Asian woman to be on a TV show in America. Kim's English was improving a lot, allowing her to deliver short speeches for many other college students.

**(the link to watch Kim's appearance on the show *What's My Line?:* https://www.youtube.com/watch?v=AGOcGmMClYc&t=186s)

Chapter 5
Kim Joins the Ninety-Nines, the International Organization of Women Pilots in the United States and Federal Aeronautics International (FAI)

When Kim gained her civil aviators' license in 1958 in the United States, she was contacted by Ms. Smith, the secretary of the International Organization of Women Pilots called The Ninety-Nines, Inc. She told Kim about the non-profit organization that had been founded in 1929 in New York to educate and promote the advancement of aviation among women pilots with a passion for flying.

Kim also came to learn in detail from Ms. Smith about the first president of the Ninety-Nines, Amelia Earhart, who was the first American female pilot to make successful solo flights, not only between Hawaii and the US mainland, but across the Atlantic Ocean as well. Kim was enamored by Amelia's life story, which she believed resembled her own.

Both Amelia and Kim were brave enough to push forward with their dreams and passion. With their minds set on their dreams to fly, nothing was impossible. Kim found herself in tears, thinking about the sad days when her parents had opposed her dream. The day she'd run away from her small room where her parents had locked her inside felt like yesterday in Kim's mind, and now she was standing much closer to her dream than anyone had ever imagined.

From then on, Kim belonged to the Ninety-Nines' International Organization of Women Pilots. Back then, Kim had little imagined that she would be able to donate her personal flying memorabilia someday to the Ninety-Nines' Museum of Women Pilots three decades later. Even though she had started the unbelievable journey of pursuing her dream with insurmountable determination, what she had experienced in someone else's country was much more than she could ever have visualized in her mind. Today, in the museum located on Amelia Earhart Lane in Oklahoma City, is a section for Kim's exhibit as the only Korean woman pilot.

As the only woman pilot to serve in the air force of the Republic of Korea during the Korean War, Kim also became recognized by the Federal Aeronautics International (FAI). FAI was founded in 1905 in Paris, France, for the purpose of promoting air sports and activities among licensed pilots around the world. Kim was thrilled to be a part of the international organization but felt a huge responsibility and burden at the same time because she was representing her mother country as the only South Korean woman pilot. The ember of her zeal for flying further and bringing what she had learned to her homeland was kindled every single day.

Chapter 6
Kim Brings Home Piper Colt

Four years had passed since Kim had come to America in 1958, and it seemed to her there was nothing more she could achieve. However, Kim had not forgotten even for a day the reason she was in the United States. Kim had to learn about the advanced development of civil aviation, not only for herself to become a good pilot with all theoretical and practical capability, but also to bring the knowledge she had obtained to her motherland, the Republic of Korea.

Once Kim had completed her language education program at Guilford along with her four years of flight training, she was prepared to fly back home, but one thing was still lingering in her mind. She had thought about bringing home an airplane, which seemed impossible because Kim did not have money to buy one. When she was interviewed by magazines, she told the reporters about her dream to purchase a light plane and bring it to her home country. The reporters laughed at her dream, saying it was wishful thinking. Kim said to herself, *No, it is not just my wish. I will certainly make it come true. I will prove myself that you are wrong.*

Kim was invited to many colleges and nonprofit organizations as a guest speaker. She was not just the talk of the town in Greensboro, North Carolina, anymore. Her life story had spread further and had drawn the attention of about ten thousand licensed women pilots, who were the members of the Ninety-Nines in the United States. They read Kim's interviews and started the fundraising to purchase a light plane for her to bring home under the slogan of "We help Captain Kim from Korea." The money that Kim and those women pilots had earned out of delivering speeches nationwide was not enough to help Kim buy an aircraft. Another huge source that could be of help in this campaign was S & H Green Stamps.

S & H Green Stamps were popular among Americans in those days to be used in buying gifts or small everyday appliances. It was an unprecedented idea for women pilots to collect and save S & H Green Stamps to buy a small airplane. They thought at first it would take at least a few years, but in just three months and seventeen days they had saved three million stamps. The members of the Ninety-Nines were ready to buy a brand-new Piper Colt airplane and donate it to Korea's Captain Kim.

Piper Aircraft, a company that manufactured civil utility airplanes, heard the news about the fundraising for Kim. The company was impressed by the story of the brave young Asian woman pilot from the country that had just gotten out of a war less than seven years ago. They decided to offer a gift of their best-selling light aircraft, the Piper Colt, to Kim. Kim felt as if she was walking on clouds, not flying over them! The American women pilots advised Kim to purchase all different kinds of options to be installed on the aircraft with her additional funds.

Kim was full of inexpressible emotions and deep gratitude. Snapshots of her past came rushing into her mind: her childhood as a small and malnourished girl in a rural town in North Korea, moving all the way to South Korea with her parents and eight siblings, the tough years in the air force academy, being the only female cadet left in the academy after the Korean War, studying and training abroad in America, appearing on a well-known TV show, joining the historic organization of women pilots founded by the legendary Amelia Earhart, and now obtaining a light airplane to bring home. Kim felt blessed and thought about all the support and care from these warmhearted women pilots and people who showed her their deep affection toward her in America. She was shedding tears of joy and gratitude and had a firm conviction that she would spend the rest of her life paving the path in the skies of her home country for more female pilots to fly.

Chapter 7
Kim Comes Back home with Piper Colt

Kim returned home in 1963 and donated her Piper Colt airplane to the South Korean government. Many thoughts and emotions filled her heart when she arrived. As a student on the special government scholarship, she was not only grateful for the once-in-a-lifetime opportunity to study abroad and the trust in her, but also took pride in her achievements in America and in gaining international recognition.

One issue that still needed to be resolved in Kim's life was the relationship with her parents. For all those years, Kim had felt sadly estranged from her stubborn parents who had not approved her future dream to become a pilot. Even with her glorious return to her home country, she did not feel at home without her parents' welcoming hugs.

Kim's sisters and brothers set up a family gathering to celebrate her successful homecoming. Kim was more than happy to see her parents waiting there at the family party with big smiles on their faces. In her parents' open arms, Kim finally felt warm and relieved—like the little ugly duckling who came back to its mom and dad after a long journey away from the nest. Her parents' teary eyes were quietly telling Kim that there was no place like home, even for a pilot who always dreamt of soaring into the sky.

Since the Republic of Korea was in a barren state when it came to the field of civil aviation, Kim started a tour, delivering speeches about what she had learned in America and how to promote civil aviation throughout the nation.

In the meantime, Kim had continued practicing flights with a police aeronautical instructor named B. M. Lee. Lee was a stern and quiet instructor. He would not wear a hint of smile or greet her with kind words. Kim would think she had made some mistakes or a critical gaffe during practice that made the instructor mad. He never laughed at any jokes Kim made, even after the training was over. Later on, she found out that Lee was too nervous to smile or laugh sitting right next to Captain Kim. They dated and fell in love, flying together for two years. The aircraft contrail in the sky had led to the aisle of their wedding in 1965.

Chapter 8
Kim Becomes a Mother

On March 15, 1965, Kim got married to the serious-looking B. M. Lee. Kim had not known this pilot instructor could also be all smiles when he was sitting next to her in the aircraft up there in the sky. He looked like the happiest man on earth on their wedding day. Back in the mid 1960s in Korea, a woman over the age of thirty might be considered somewhat old to be a bride. Kim was thirty one when she married Lee, but age did not matter to this couple. They felt like they were a perfect match made above the clouds!

Kim and Lee had their first child in the spring of 1966—a daughter. Since Kim had returned to Korea, she had been invited by many different organizations and conferences to be a guest speaker, but outside of those scheduled events, she tried to stay home most of the time, taking care of her newborn baby. Singing a lullaby to her daughter while feeding or giving her a bath were the happiest moments in Kim's life.

Then came a day when she was scheduled to take her first official solo flight overseas in 1967. She had to fly in a light airplane to Tokyo, Japan, for the purpose of enhancing friendship and goodwill between South Korea and Japan. Just as she used to do as a pilot, Kim was facing the most difficult moment before taking off. Looking at her baby sleeping nearby, she was putting her fingernail clippings and locks of hair in an envelope. Most of all, Kim's mind was full of concerns and sadness, leaving a message that could be her final words for her husband and their precious daughter. This mind-boggling ritual before each flight continued until her second daughter was born in 1969.

Kim's message for her two daughters that she would leave before each flight always read like this:

"Dearest my girls, Boyoung and Jiyoung,

Mom is out to fly. Even if I do not come back home to you as early as you expect, do not cry. Mom is always watching over you from above the clouds. I know you will love each other, and so will mommy. Always have confidence in whatever you do, because everything in the world is all up to you. You are the only one whom you can count on."

Chapter 9
Kim's Goodwill Flight to Japan

On the day of Kim's first official solo flight to Tokyo, Japan, she was more than excited about making history with this goodwill event between nations as the first woman civilian pilot. However, in the back of her mind, Kim was reluctant to leave her baby daughter and husband behind. Taking a deep breath, Kim tried to pull herself together and clear her mind in her cockpit.

Once she made a good takeoff, nothing in the sky could distract Kim. Now at the altitude of ten thousand feet above the ground, she turned into a courageous young pilot on an important mission. Feeling completely disconnected to the world below, everything in and outside of her aircraft seemed to be perfectly smooth and peaceful just as she had planned on the airway. Sitting alone in the silent cockpit, Kim's mind was filled with her baby daughter at home. Deep in thought, she did not realize she was lost and had gradually deviated from the route to Tokyo.

The fuel indicator on the gauge was showing Kim that she was running out of fuel. Kim lost her way and was still stuck in the middle of thick clouds, trying catch a glimpse of sun. Her face was drenched with tears and sweat. For the first time in her life, Kim regretted that she'd become a pilot, a wife, and a mother. With less than eight minutes left to fly on her remaining fuel, Kim was lucky enough to get out of the clouds and made an emergency landing. From that day on, Kim never tried to fly head on and break through the clouds when her mind was focused somewhere else.

The Japanese civilian pilot Nozoki and her other fellow pilots were waiting there, along with reporters and camera crew, to welcome Kim and celebrate her successful solo flight.

Chapter 10
Kim Promotes National Women's Leadership

As a mother of two daughters, Kim often thought seriously about what women could do in a conservative society. She asked herself time and time again if Korean society was changing so that women could have equal rights and responsibilities, as men did, in a variety of fields. Her question was always the same: "Are my two daughters going to be able to live as happy members of society with equal rights to do what they desire in the future?" In the late 1960s, Korean women were not actively participating in society as workers outside the home.

Inspired by Amelia Earhart's Ninety-Nines, Inc., Kim wanted to sow the seeds for women with passion to grow, so she established the Korea Women's Civil Aviation Association. Through the funds and scholarships prepared in this association, a lot of gifted women who had dreams to fly or study aviation were given a chance to achieve their goals. Kim also played a significant role in getting the government to allow women to apply for the military academy, just as she had several decades ago.

As a woman pilot who pioneered the field in her motherland, Kim wished to kindle the light of enhancing women's rights and status in Korean society and fight discrimination against women. Kim's path crossed with the international women's club named Zonta. It is an international organization with the purpose of advancing women's rights. Through many years of volunteer activities to help talented women in need of financial support, Kim and her fellow Zonta members had been happily devoting their time and energy to women's status in Korean society. Kim became the leader of this Zonta group in Seoul, Korea, for three years until 1987, and thereafter, started the life of a women's rights activist in full swing as the chairperson of Korea National Council of Women for six years.

Chapter 11
Kim Wins the Gold Air Medal from FAI (1992) and Dongbaek Medal (2013) in Korea

Kim had been participating in the annual conference of FAI (Federal Aeronautics International) for twenty-six years. For all those years, she had not forgotten one thing: "I owe my country and all my fellow women pilots in America and around the world a lot. Without their support, I could not have stood where I am. Without their affection for me, I could not have made any contribution to improving women's status in the world of civil aviation. Without their trust in me, I could never have trusted myself." These were the main lines from her acceptance speech when she was awarded the Gold Air Medal by FAI in 1992. The purpose of awarding the Gold Air Medal by FAI was to recognize and celebrate the members who had made huge contributions to the development of aeronautics by their continuous activities and achievements to champion the cause of developing aviation in public.

In 2013, Kim became the nation's first woman pilot who had received the Medal of the Order of Civil Merit called *Dongbaek* during Women's Week in Korea. It was offered by the then Ministry of Gender Equality and Family. Kim was feeling tremendously honored and humbled to become a recognized figure and an icon of civil aviation, not only in her home country, but in the world as well. When she was standing on the pedestal to deliver her acceptance speech, her mind began to travel once again high into the sky. The sky had always been right there waiting for her to shed tears and sweat. The sky had always been and will always be where her heart is.

Printed in the United States
by Baker & Taylor Publisher Services